A. Passion For Flavor

A Passion For Flavor

COOKING WITH INFUSED VINEGAR & OIL

BY EVE PLOCIENNIK

WITH RITA RANDAZZO

A Passion For Flavor

I'M SURE YOU KNOW WHAT I MEAN BY "A PASSION FOR FLAVOR." PASSIONATE COOKS ARE NOT SATISFIED UNTIL THE FOOD THEY SERVE SINGS WITH FLAVOR, EVERY BITE A LOVE SONG TO THE RICHNESS OF LIFE.

THE QUESTION IS HOW TO ACHIEVE THAT SUPERB TASTE, HOW TO MAKE EVERY MEAL MEMORABLE, IN THE SMALL AMOUNT OF TIME WE HAVE FOR COOKING. I WROTE THIS BOOK TO ANSWER THAT QUESTION, TO SHARE WITH YOU WHAT I HAVE LEARNED IN MY 10 YEARS OF EXPLORING THE SECRETS OF GREAT FLAVOR. IN IT YOU WILL FIND RECIPES FOR BOLD SALSAS AND CHUTNEYS, MOUTH-WATERING APPETIZERS, DISTINCTIVE SALADS, SAVORY SOUPS, ELEGANT ENTREES, ENTICING SIDE DISHES, INTRIGUING SAUCES, AND DIVINE DESSERTS, ALL MADE IRRESISTIBLE BY A VERY SPECIAL FLAVOR ENHANCER.

THE DEVELOPMENT OF THIS CONDIMENT BEGAN WITH MY HERB GARDEN, AND THE DISCOVERY THAT I COULD INFUSE VINEGAR AND OLIVE OIL WITH THE INCOMPARABLE FRESH TASTE OF ALL THE LOVELY HERBS GROWING THERE. CHIVES, MINT, SAGE, BASIL, DILL, OREGANO, AND SO MANY MORE, EACH ADDED ITS OWN MAGIC TO MY CREATIONS.

HERBS WERE THE BEGINNING, BUT I WENT FURTHER IN MY EXPERIMENTATION TO FIND FLAVOR COMBINATIONS THAT WOULD CAUSE ORDINARY DISHES TO EXPLODE WITH EXCITING TASTE. I MADE RICH INFUSIONS OF OLIVE OIL AND OF WINE VINEGAR WITH HUNDREDS OF INGREDIENTS, FROM BLACK PEPPER AND RED ONION TO CRANBERRY, LIME, AND GINGER. TO MY DELIGHT, THESE MARVELOUS CONDIMENTS TURNED THE SIMPLEST MEALS INTO GOURMET FEASTS. YOU WILL BE ASTONISHED, FOR INSTANCE, BY HOW THE FAMILIAR SALAD OF SLICED TOMATO AND FRESH MOZZARELLA IS MADE FAR MORE DELICIOUS WHEN DRESSED WITH *Basil Olive Oil* !

Not only will my oil and vinegar infusions add fabulous flavor to everything you cook, but they are beautiful to look at; much too attractive to tuck away in a cupboard. I have applied all I have learned through my studies in fine arts to design the most colorful, most eye-appealing combinations that satisfy the desire for beauty, as well as an appetite for tasty meals.

Once you have stocked your kitchen with a collection of flavored vinegars and oils, using them is as easy as adding a dash of Zesty Dill Vinegar to your homemade lentil soup, or tossing hot pasta with heady Porcini Mushroom Oil and grated Romano cheese. But don't stop there, because I hope you will experience the pleasure of trying my recipes for unique dishes like Asparagus & Toasted Hazelnuts, Zesty Dill Crab Cakes with Cantaloupe Pineapple Salsa, Cherry Pecan Chutney, and Oriental Lacquered Chicken, each one singing with the flavor of my vinegar and olive oil creations.

In all, this book contains a decade's worth of discoveries: over 70 of my favorite recipes for making the most of infused oils and vinegars, the secret flavor enhancers for today's busy cook. I know you will enjoy rave reviews from your family and guests when they taste the exquisite meals you make with these unique condiments!

Eve Plociennik

TABLE OF CONTENTS

Chutneys, Relishes & Salsas

Avocado Lime & Tomato Salsa 13
Three Bean Salsa 13
Cherry Pecan Chutney 14
Green Tomato & Cilantro Relish 14
Fresh Cranberry Relish 15
Cantaloupe-Pineapple Salsa..15
Rhubarb & Kumquat Chutney 16
Three Pepper Chutney 16
Pear & Apple Chutney...17

Appetizers

Fresh Garden Tomatoes 20
Tuna Caponata..23
Fresh Chili Ginger Dip 24
Smoked Salmon Spread 26
Dilled Cucumber Yogurt Dip......................................26
Black Olive Tapenade 26
Vegetable Antipasto..28
Spicy Deviled Eggs..30
Stuffed Cherry Tomatoes 30
Citrus Cucumber Sandwiches 30
Chilled Salmon Tart 33
Spinach Mushroom Tart 34
Shrimp & Vegetable Kebabs 37
Texas Style Spicy Chicken Wings 38
Salmon Stuffed Rice Balls...40
Stuffed Mushrooms Florentine 42

Salads

Basic Vinaigrette 47
Tomatoes And Basil 48
Tossed Salmon Salad..51
Sliced Orange Beet Salad 52
Fresh Fennel Salad 55
Peppers Tricolore...56

Chilled Tortellini & Olive Salad 58
Summer Beet Salad 61
Fresh Tomatoes and Mozzarella Salad 62
Mixed Bean And Salmon Salad 65
Panzanella..............................66
Greek Island Salad 69
Warm Spinach Salad 70
Grilled Vegetable Pasta Salad 73
Pear & Blue Cheese Salad 74
Shrimp & Salmon Salad 76

Entrees
& Side Dishes

Salmon Asparagus Pasta 80
Gazpacho..............................83
Tomato & Orange Soup 85
Roasted Red Pepper Linguine 86
Lamb Ragù 89
Penne & Black Olives 90
Goat Cheese & Proscuitto Spaghettini 93
Farfalle 94
Robust Chili Tomato Sauce Over Rotini 96
Basil Scented Tuna..............................99
Zesty Dill Crab Cakes 100
Caribbean Lime Ginger Tuna..............................102
Savory Shrimp 104
Oriental Lacquered Chicken 107
Savory Stuffed Tomatoes 107
Roasted Rainbow Peppers 109
Baked Chili Rice 109
Asparagus And Toasted Hazelnuts..........................110
Beef Tenderloins..............................110
Herbed Pork Roast 112
Spicy Red Cabbage 112
Mashed Potatoes & Herbs 112

Desserts

Apple Cranberry Crisp..............................116
Eve's Sweet Citrus Pecan Pie 119
Tangy Watermelon 120
Citrus Scented Pound Cake 123
Raspberry Mint Cooler 124
Fresh Cherry Pie 127

The Flavorful Pantry

*I*MAGINE HAVING A KITCHEN FULL OF INSTANT FLAVOR POTIONS THAT WILL TURN YOUR HUMBLEST DINNER INTO A FANTASTIC EPICUREAN FEAST.

WHEN YOU HAVE A SELECTION OF INFUSED VINEGAR AND OIL ON HAND, YOUR EVERYDAY RECIPES WILL TAKE ON VIBRANT NEW LIFE WITH TANTALIZING LAYERS OF FLAVOR. YOU'LL WONDER HOW YOU EVER COOKED WITHOUT THEM!

THANKS TO THE EXCITING ARRAY OF FLAVORED OLIVE OILS AND VINEGARS AVAILABLE TODAY, EVEN THE BUSIEST AMONG US CAN COOK LIKE A GOURMET WITHOUT A LOT OF WORK. THE SUBTLE NUANCES OF GREAT TASTE ARE BUILT RIGHT IN, SO YOU NEED NOT CHOP FRESH HERBS FOR THE SALAD DRESSING OR SAUTE GARLIC IN OIL FOR A SPAGHETTI SAUCE.

BEFORE I TELL YOU THE SECRETS OF MAKING MY PIQUANT VINEGARS, LET ME URGE YOU TO EXPERIMENT ON YOUR OWN ONCE YOU HAVE MASTERED THE BASIC TECHNIQUES FOR MAKING FLAVORED VINEGAR. THE CREATIVE POSSIBILITIES ARE LIMITLESS, SO ALLOW YOURSELF TO BE INSPIRED BY YOUR GARDEN, THE NEIGHBORHOOD FARM STAND, OR THE PRODUCE COUNTER AT THE SUPERMARKET.

HERBS AND SPICES, FRUITS AND VEGETABLES, EVEN ROSES AND LAVENDER: TRY THEM ALL! AND WHAT ABOUT VANILLA BEANS, COCONUT, HORSERADISH, LEMONGRASS, WALNUTS? PERHAPS IF I LIVE ANOTHER 100 YEARS I WILL RUN OUT OF IDEAS TO EXPERIMENT WITH.

FOR OVER FIVE CENTURIES COOKS HAVE USED VINEGAR AND OILS TO FLAVOR THEIR FOOD. I HAVE BEEN ABLE TO MAKE MY OWN CONTRIBUTION OVER 10 YEARS OF WORK ON GOURMET ART OF VERMONT'S ELEGANT OIL AND VINEGAR SPECIALTIES. I'D LIKE TO SHARE WITH YOU SOME OF WHAT I HAVE LEARNED, TO HELP YOU CREATE YOUR OWN DISTINCTIVE INFUSIONS.

Eve's Helpful Hints

I AM CAREFUL TO ALWAYS USE WHITE WINE AND CHAMPAGNE VINEGARS IMPORTED FROM FRANCE BECAUSE THEIR SUPERIOR CLARITY SHOWS OFF THE BEAUTY OF THE RED PEPPERS, YELLOW LEMON SLICES, LOVELY SPRIGS OF HERBS, AND ALL THE OTHER SHAPELY, COLORFUL INGREDIENTS THAT GO INTO PREPARING MY FLAVORED VINEGAR SPECIALTIES.

BE SURE TO READ THE LABEL BEFORE YOU BUY. VINEGAR USED FOR MAKING INFUSIONS MUST HAVE AN ACETIC ACID CONTENT OF 7% OR HIGHER AND SHOULD BE IDENTIFIED AS "AGED" VINEGAR.

SELECT ONLY THE FINEST QUALITY, FRESH INGREDIENTS FOR ALL YOUR INFUSIONS AND USE THEM AS SOON AS POSSIBLE AFTER HARVESTING. HERBS SHOULD HAVE NO DARK SPOTS, FRUITS AND VEGETABLES NO BRUISES. REMEMBER, THE FINISHED CREATION CAN TASTE NO BETTER THAN THE INGREDIENTS THAT GO INTO IT.

DO NOT FAIL TO STERILIZE BOTTLES AND JARS BEFORE MAKING YOUR INFUSIONS, AND SEAL VINEGAR WITH NONMETALLIC LIDS THAT ARE NON-REACTIVE WITH ACID. GLASS OR CORK STOPPERS ARE GOOD CHOICES; CORKS FROM A WINE SUPPLY SHOP ARE PRE-STERILIZED.

SINCE FLAVORED VINEGAR IN A PRETTY BOTTLE MAKES SUCH AN EXCELLENT GIFT, DO KEEP YOUR EYES OPEN FOR DECORATIVE BOTTLES AT FLEA MARKETS AND ANTIQUE STORES, OR BUY FANCY BOTTLES WITH ATTACHED CERAMIC STOPPERS AT A KITCHEN SUPPLY SHOP. INCLUDE A RECIPE WITH YOUR GIFT CARD, SO YOUR FRIEND WILL KNOW HOW TO USE THIS DELICIOUS CONDIMENT.

AS YOU USE THE VINEGAR INFUSIONS, TOP OFF THE BOTTLE WITH MORE BEST-QUALITY WHITE WINE OR CHAMPAGNE VINEGAR. YOU'LL NEVER RUN OUT OF YOUR FAVORITE FLAVOR ENHANCER!

The Flavorful Recipes

THE INFLUENCES ON MY COOKING HAVE BEEN BOTH WIDE AND DEEP, LIKE THE OCEAN I CROSSED TO GET TO AMERICA.

I GREW UP IN POLAND, WHERE MY FAMILY OFTEN ENTERTAINED VISITORS FROM OTHER EUROPEAN COUNTRIES. WHEN THEY PREPARED THEIR NATIVE DISHES I WATCHED AND LEARNED, FASCINATED BY THE VARIED CUISINES OF GERMANY, FRANCE, AND GREECE. I ALWAYS WANTED TO KNOW HOW THESE COOKS ACHIEVED THEIR UNIQUE FLAVORINGS AND WAS FOREVER ASKING OUR GUESTS FOR THEIR SECRETS.

LATER MY HUSBAND AND I LEFT POLAND WITH $100 BORROWED FROM MY FATHER AND FLED TO GERMANY, WHERE WE LIVED AS REFUGEES WHILE AWAITING A SPONSORSHIP FOR AMERICA. AGAIN I HAD AN OPPORTUNITY TO STUDY THE DISTINCTIVE DISHES OF A FOREIGN LAND, BECAUSE WE WERE SENT TO LIVE WITH A DOCTOR WHOSE WIFE WAS THE MOST MAGNIFICENT COOK.

SHE MADE EVERY DINNER SEEM LIKE A PARTY! EACH COURSE WAS PERFECTLY SEASONED AND BEAUTIFULLY PRESENTED, AND I VOWED THEN TO ALWAYS REMEMBER HOW ATTENTION TO DETAIL CAN EXPRESS LOVE AND HOSPITALITY.

WHEN KRIS AND I FINALLY REACHED AMERICA I KNEW ONLY 50 ENGLISH WORDS, CAN YOU IMAGINE? AND YET, I FOUND, THE LANGUAGE OF COOKING IS THE SAME EVERYWHERE. IT WAS IN CALIFORNIA, THAT I TRULY FELL IN LOVE WITH FOOD, WITH ITS EXUBERANCE, ITS PASSION, AND THE SHEER SENSUALITY OF CONSUMING THE DELICIOUS FLAVORS.

ALL THROUGH MY TRAVELS I COLLECTED THE RECIPES OF OUTSTANDING COOKS AND WORKED OUT OTHER PREPARATIONS IN MY OWN KITCHEN TO DUPLICATE THE WONDERFUL DISHES I HAD ENJOYED ON MY CULINARY ODYSSEY. EVERY RECIPE HAS BENEFITED FROM THE INCLUSION OF MY FLAVORED OILS AND VINEGAR! YOU WILL DISCOVER HOW THESE USEFUL AND BEAUTIFUL CONDIMENTS WILL ENHANCE YOUR OWN RECIPES, TOO.

13

Avocado Lime & Tomato Salsa

3 TABLESPOONS GINGER LIME VINEGAR
1 MEDIUM RED ONION, FINELY CHOPPED
4 TOMATOES, PEELED AND SEEDED
1 AVOCADO
SALT AND FRESHLY GROUND PEPPER

In a medium bowl, mix the vinegar and the onion.
Dice the tomatoes and add to the bowl. Quarter the avocado. Remove the stone and skin,
then dice the flesh. Add to the bowl and toss carefully. Cover and chill until ready to serve.

Three Bean Salsa

1 ENVELOPE SAVORY HERB WITH GARLIC
   SOUP MIX
1/4 CUP WATER
1 LARGE TOMATO, CHOPPED
1 CUP CANNED CANNELLINI OR RED KIDNEY BEANS,
   DRAINED
1 CUP CANNED BLACK BEANS OR PINTO BEANS, DRAINED
1 CUP CANNED CHICK-PEAS OR GARBANZO BEANS, DRAINED
2 TEASPOONS THYME-LEMON VINEGAR

Pour the soup mix and the water into a saucepan. Bring to a boil over high heat. Reduce
heat to low and stir in the tomato. Simmer 3 minutes. Stir in beans and simmer 3 more
minutes until heated through. Stir in the vinegar. Garnish with chopped parsley or
cilantro, if desired.

Cherry Pecan Chutney

1 POUND DRIED PEACHES, FINELY CHOPPED
1/3 CUP DRIED CHERRIES
1/4 CUP GRAND MARNIER LIQUEUR
1 RED BELL PEPPER, FINELY CHOPPED
1 APPLE, PEELED, CORED, AND FINELY CHOPPED
3/4 CUP BROWN SUGAR
1/2 CUP CITRUS DELIGHT VINEGAR
1/4 CUP WATER
1/2 TEASPOON GROUND CINNAMON
1/8 TEASPOON GROUND CLOVES
1 TEASPOON MUSTARD SEED
1 TEASPOON NUTMEG
1/2 TEASPOON CAYENNE
1/4 CUP FINELY CHOPPED TOASTED PECANS

Plump the peaches and cherries in Grand Marnier for 1 hour. Put all of the ingredients in a heavy saucepan, including the peach mixture. Bring the mixture to a boil, stirring well to dissolve the sugar. Reduce the heat and let cook until the mixture begins to thicken, about 20 to 30 minutes. Remove the chutney from the heat. Let cool and put into jars with tight-fitting lids. Refrigerate.

Green Tomato & Cilantro Relish

2 1/2 POUNDS GREEN TOMATOES, CHOPPED
1 LARGE CUCUMBER, CHOPPED
1 RED BELL PEPPER, CHOPPED
2 TABLESPOONS SALT
3 GARLIC CLOVES, CHOPPED
3 CUPS THYME-LEMON VINEGAR
1/2 CUP MAPLE SYRUP
1 TABLESPOON WHOLE GRAIN MUSTARD
2 TABLESPOONS ITALIAN PARSLEY, CHOPPED

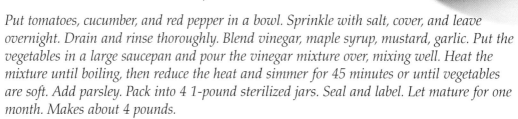

Put tomatoes, cucumber, and red pepper in a bowl. Sprinkle with salt, cover, and leave overnight. Drain and rinse thoroughly. Blend vinegar, maple syrup, mustard, garlic. Put the vegetables in a large saucepan and pour the vinegar mixture over, mixing well. Heat the mixture until boiling, then reduce the heat and simmer for 45 minutes or until vegetables are soft. Add parsley. Pack into 4 1-pound sterilized jars. Seal and label. Let mature for one month. Makes about 4 pounds.

Fresh Cranberry Relish

4 CUPS FRESH CRANBERRIES
2 ORANGES, PEELED AND SECTIONED
1/2 CUP RAISINS
1/2 CUP CHOPPED WALNUTS
1 1/4 CUP SUGAR
1/4 TEASPOON GINGER
1/4 TEASPOON CINNAMON
2 TABLESPOONS ORANGE JUICE
2 TABLESPOONS CRANBERRY ORANGE VINEGAR

In a 3 quart casserole, combine all ingredients, mixing well.
Cover with waxed paper and microwave on high 9 - 11 minutes or until the berries burst
and the liquid is slightly thickened, stirring every 4 minutes. Refrigerate. Makes 4 cups.

15

Cantaloupe-Pineapple Salsa

1/2 CANTALOUPE, SEEDED, RIND REMOVED AND DICED
1/2 SMALL RIPE PINEAPPLE, RIND REMOVED, CORED
  AND DICED
3 SCALLIONS, FINELY CHOPPED
2 TABLESPOONS PARSLEY
2 TABLESPOONS ZESTY DILL VINEGAR

Prepare the Salsa by combining the cantaloupe, pineapple,
scallions, parsley, and vinegar in a small bowl. Refrigerate, covered,
for 3 hours or up to 2 days. Bring to room temperature before using.

Rhubarb & Kumquat Chutney

3 POUNDS RHUBARB
3/4 POUND KUMQUATS, SEEDED AND CHOPPED
3 LARGE ONIONS, CHOPPED
3 1/2 CUPS CRANBERRY ORANGE VINEGAR
1 TEASPOON ORANGE ZEST
1 1/2 CUPS LIGHT BROWN SUGAR
1 1/2 CUPS GOLDEN RAISINS
1 TABLESPOON WHITE PEPPERCORNS
1 TEASPOON ALLSPICE

Put the rhubarb into a deep pan with onions, vinegar, zest, brown sugar and raisins. Simmer slowly, stirring occasionally, until brown sugar has dissolved. Tie spices into a small square of cheesecloth and put in the pan along with the kumquats. Continue simmering until thick. Discard the spices and pack the chutney into sterilized jars. Seal and label. Let mature for 2 weeks. Makes about 7 pounds.

Three Pepper Chutney

1 1/2 YELLOW BELL PEPPER
1 1/2 RED BELL PEPPER
1 LARGE ONION, DICED
3/4 CUP LIGHT BROWN SUGAR
1/2 CUP GINGER-LIME VINEGAR
1/4 CUP WATER
2 GREEN SERRANO PEPPERS, SEEDED AND CHOPPED
2 TABLESPOONS CHOPPED PARSLEY
2 CLOVES GARLIC, MINCED
1 TEASPOON DRY MUSTARD
1/3 CUP TOASTED PINE NUTS

Combine all ingredients except pine nuts in a medium saucepan. Bring to a boil, then reduce heat and simmer until tender, about 15 minutes. Stir in pine nuts. Chill at least 12 hours before serving. Makes 4 cups.

Pear & Apple Chutney

4 CUPS GOLDEN DELICIOUS APPLES, PEELED, CORED AND
   CUT INTO 1/2 INCH SLICES
4 CUPS FIRM PEARS, PEELED, CORED AND CUT INTO
   1/2-INCH SLICES
ZEST AND JUICE OF 2 LEMONS
6 CUPS CITRUS DELIGHT VINEGAR
2 LARGE ONIONS, PEELED AND CHOPPED
4 GARLIC CLOVES, PEELED AND MINCED
2 TABLESPOONS SALT
2 TABLESPOONS MUSTARD SEED
3 TABLESPOONS GRATED FRESH GINGER
1 TEASPOON CAYENNE PEPPER
1 TEASPOON GROUND CINNAMON
2 CUPS LIGHT BROWN SUGAR
5 CUPS RAISINS
4 CUPS WALNUTS, CHOPPED

17

Place fruit in a large bowl, cover with cold water and the juice of 2 lemons. Set aside. In a large nonreactive kettle, combine the vinegar with 2 cups cold water, lemon zest, onions, garlic, salt and spices and bring to a boil over high heat. Reduce the heat and simmer for 15 minutes, or until the onion is translucent. Add the brown and granulated sugars and fruit and bring to a boil. Lower the heat and simmer for 1 hour, stirring occasionally to prevent scorching. When the chutney has thickened, add the raisins and nuts and cook for another 15 minutes or until thick. The chutney will continue to thicken as it cools. Ladle the chutney into sterilized hot pint or half-pint jars, leaving approximately 1/4- inch headspace. Seal jars with canning lids according to manufacturer's directions and process in a boiling water bath for 10 minutes. Cool, tighten lids, and store. Or, cover tightly and keep in the refrigerator up to 3 weeks.

Fresh Garden Tomatoes
with Italian Vinaigrette

The sunny flavors of Provence are here, in ripe red tomatoes with warm anchovy and garlic dressing. A traditional preparation enlivened by the delicious herbal taste of an Italian Garden, this recipe is one you will make over and over again.

2 TABLESPOONS ITALIAN GARDEN OLIVE OIL
1 MEDIUM CLOVE GARLIC, MINCED
5 ANCHOVY FILLETS, COARSELY CHOPPED
4 MEDIUM TOMATOES, CUT INTO EIGHTHS
SALT AND FRESHLY GROUND PEPPER TO TASTE
2 TABLESPOONS PARSLEY, CHOPPED
1 TEASPOON ITALIAN GARDEN VINEGAR

Heat the olive oil and garlic in a small skillet over low heat. Stir in the anchovies, and cook about 1 minute. Place the tomato wedges in a serving dish, and sprinkle lightly with vinegar, salt, and pepper. Pour the warm dressing over the tomatoes, add the parsley, and toss well to coat. Serve immediately.

Tuna Caponata
with Pesto & Basil Olive Oil

Caponata is often described as the Italian ratatouille, but my version is very different, influenced by the unique flavor combinations I so enjoyed in California. Tuna replaces the usual eggplant, and the pesto-flavored dressing is sublime. Serve it with good crusty bread at the start of a big Italian feast.

2 TABLESPOONS PLUS 3/4 CUP BASIL OLIVE OIL
3 LARGE ONIONS, CHOPPED
6 OUNCES ANCHOVIES, DRAINED AND FINELY CHOPPED
6 CUPS CHUNKY ITALIAN STYLE SPAGHETTI SAUCE
12 OUNCES TUNA PACKED IN WATER, DRAINED
3/4 CUP PESTO VINEGAR
6 LARGE CLOVES GARLIC, MINCED
3/4 CUP PARSLEY, CHOPPED
10 OUNCES SMALL CAPERS, DRAINED
2 1/2 CUPS BLACK OLIVES, PITTED, SLICED
SALT AND FRESHLY GROUND PEPPER TO TASTE

Heat 2 tablespoons of the olive oil in a large saucepan. Stir in onions and saute over medium heat until limp, about 8 to 10 minutes. Add anchovies and tomato sauce and simmer, partially covered, for 10 minutes. Combine tuna, vinegar, olive oil, garlic, parsley, capers and olives in a large bowl. Stir in tomato sauce, season with salt and pepper. Chill until serving.

24

Fresh Chili Ginger Dip
with Hot Pepper Olive Oil

This is a cocktail sauce for the brave! Fiery hot with fresh chili and Pepper olive oil, it has an Asian flavor imparted by the soy sauce, ginger and Ginger Lime vinegar.

1 SMALL RED CHILI, HALVED, SEEDS REMOVED, CHOPPED

1 INCH PIECE FRESH GINGER, CHOPPED

2 GARLIC CLOVES

1 TEASPOON MUSTARD POWDER

1 TABLESPOON CHILI SAUCE

2 TEASPOONS Hot Pepper OLIVE OIL

2 TEASPOONS LIGHT SOY SAUCE

4 TABLESPOONS Ginger Lime VINEGAR

2 TABLESPOONS CHOPPED FRESH PARSLEY

SALT AND PEPPER TO TASTE

Crush the chili, ginger, garlic and mustard powder to a paste, using a mortar and pestle. In a bowl, mix together all the remaining ingredients except the parsley. Add the paste and blend well. Cover and chill for 24 hours. Stir in the parsley and season to taste. Serve in a small individual bowl with chilled cooked shrimp.

Smoked Salmon Spread

4 TABLESPOONS ITALIAN GARDEN OLIVE OIL
2 - 3 TABLESPOONS CITRUS DELIGHT VINEGAR
2 TEASPOONS THYME, CHOPPED
PINCH OF CAYENNE PEPPER
4 OUNCES SALMON, POACHED, SKINNED, BONED, AND FLAKED
2 OUNCES SMOKED SALMON, CHOPPED
SALT AND FRESHLY GROUND BLACK PEPPER TO TASTE

Combine the olive oil, vinegar, and thyme. Season with salt, pepper and cayenne to taste. Mash in the cooked salmon- do not make it too smooth- and the smoked salmon. Serve with bread or toast.

Dilled Cucumber Yogurt Dip

16 OUNCES (2 CUPS) NONFAT YOGURT
1 SEEDLESS CUCUMBER, PEELED AND CUT INTO 1/2 INCH PIECES
2 CLOVES GARLIC, MINCED
1/4 CUP FRESH DILL
1 TABLESPOON ITALIAN GARDEN OLIVE OIL
2 TABLESPOONS ZESTY DILL VINEGAR
1/2 TEASPOON SALT
1/4 TEASPOON FRESHLY GROUND PEPPER

Line colander with a double thickness of cheesecloth. Add yogurt, and drain for 2 hours in the refrigerator. Remove yogurt from refrigerator, and combine with cucumber, garlic, and dill in small bowl. Stir in oil, vinegar, salt and pepper. Refrigerate, covered with plastic, until thick and smooth, at least 1 hour or up to 2 days.

Black Olive Tapenade

10 OUNCES SMALL BLACK OLIVES,
  PITTED, CHOPPED
2 ANCHOVY FILLETS
2 CLOVES OF GARLIC, PEELED
1 TEASPOON DIJON MUSTARD

3 TEASPOONS CAPERS
1 1/2 TABLESPOONS THYME LEMON VINEGAR
FRESHLY GROUND BLACK PEPPER
5 TABLESPOONS OLIVE OIL

Put all the ingredients except the olive oil into a blender and process for 1 minute. Slowly add the olive oil and continue processing until you have a smooth paste. Place in a serving bowl and accompany with french bread.

Vegetable Antipasto
with Italian Vinaigrette

1/4 CUP PLUS 3 TABLESPOONS ITALIAN GARDEN OLIVE OIL
6 BELL PEPPERS, HALVED LENGTHWISE, STEM, MEMBRANES AND SEEDS REMOVED
1 1/2 POUNDS EGGPLANT, SLICED IN 1/4-INCH-THICK ROUNDS
3 SMALL ZUCCHINI, ENDS TRIMMED, CUT IN 1/4-INCH-THICK SLICES
1 POUND MUSHROOMS, WIPED CLEAN AND SLICED
1/3 CUP ITALIAN GARDEN VINEGAR
2 TABLESPOONS FRESH LEMON JUICE
1/2 CUP FRESH MINT, COARSELY CHOPPED
1/2 CUP BASIL, COARSELY CHOPPED
1 TEASPOON SALT
1/2 TEASPOON GROUND FRESH PEPPER
8 CUPS SALAD GREENS
OIL-CURED OLIVES

Heat broiler. Brush 2 jelly-roll pans or cookie sheets with 1/2 tablespoon of the oil. Place pepper halves on broiler-pan rack, cut sides down. Broil 4 to 5 inches from heat source for 12 to 15 minutes until skins are mostly charred. Remove peppers to a saucepan and cover. Turn off broiler. Preheat oven to 425 degrees F. Arrange eggplant rounds on prepared pans in a single layer. Brush with 2 tablespoons olive oil. Roast, turning eggplant slices over after 10 minutes. Roast 8 to 10 minutes longer or until soft. Remove slices to a large bowl. Meanwhile bring a 3-quart pot of water to boil. Add zucchini and boil 5 to 7 minutes until tender. Drain, rinse under cold water and pat dry. Add to eggplant. Pull charred skin from peppers. Cut halves lengthwise in quarters. Add to bowl with vegetables. Add mushrooms, vinegar, remaining 1/4 cup oil, lemon juice, mint and basil. Salt and pepper to taste. Toss to coat; let stand at room temperature 30 minutes, or cover and refrigerate up to 1 day. To serve, bring vegetables to room temperature. Line a large serving platter with salad greens. Carefully remove vegetables from bowl and arrange in groups on the greens. Scatter olives over vegetables. Sprinkle with remaining basil and mint.

Spicy Deviled Eggs

8 EGGS, HARD-COOKED

2 TABLESPOONS CREAM CHEESE, AT ROOM TEMPERATURE

2 TABLESPOONS HOT PEPPER OLIVE OIL

1 TEASPOON CURRY POWDER

1 TABLESPOON SIMPLE PEPPER VINEGAR

SALT AND FRESHLY GROUND PEPPER

Shell the eggs and cut them in half lengthwise. Remove the yolks and put into the work bowl of a food processor fitted with a metal blade or into a blender. Set the egg whites aside. Add the cream cheese, olive oil, curry powder, vinegar, and salt and pepper to the food processor. Process at medium speed until you have a thick mixture, about 1 minute. Fill the egg-white halves with the yolk mixture, using enough of the mixture to round the top so that it looks like the original egg shape. Arrange tbe stuffed eggs on a large, flat plate. Keep in a cool place until ready to serve.

Stuffed Cherry Tomatoes

20 CHERRY TOMATOES

12 OUNCES OF GOAT'S MILK CHEESE

2 TABLESPOONS ITALIAN GARDEN OLIVE OIL

2 GREEN ONIONS, FINELY CHOPPED

1 TABLESPOON FRESH PARSLEY

FRESHLY GROUND PEPPER

Cut a small cap from the top of each tomato. With a small spoon scoop out the flesh. Invert the hollowed-out tomatoes on a plate to drain. Place the cheese in a bowl and mash with a fork. Add the olive oil, onions, parsley and pepper. Mix well. Fill the tomatoes with the stuffing. Serve the tomatoes cold.

Citrus Cucumber Sandwiches

CITRUS MAYONNAISE:

1/3 CUP LOW-FAT MAYONNAISE

1 TABLESPOON FINELY CHOPPED DILL

1 TEASPOON FRESH LIME JUICE

2 TEASPOONS ZESTY DILL VINEGAR

3/4 TEASPOON SUGAR

DASH FRESHLY GROUND PEPPER

18 SLICES VERY THIN, FIRM WHITE BREAD, CUT IN 36 2-INCH ROUNDS WITH A COOKIE CUTTER

1 LONG CUCUMBER, THINLY SLICED INTO 36 ROUNDS

1 SMALL CARROT, FINELY SHREDDED

1 TABLESPOON PECANS, FINELY CHOPPED

In a small bowl whisk citrus mayonnaise ingredients until well blended. Spread mayonnaise mixture on 1 side of bread rounds. Top with a cucumber slice and arrange on a platter. Top each sandwich with a pinch of shredded carrot and a sprinkling of chopped nuts.

Chilled Salmon Tart

with Zesty Dill Vinaigrette

I love this recipe because it is so easy to prepare and so pretty with the pink salmon and cool green cucumber garnish. The tart is served cold, as a light luncheon dish or impressive appetizer.

1/4 Zesty Dill vinegar
2 teaspoons unflavored gelatin
7 tablespoons plain yogurt
7 tablespoons mayonnaise
Salt and pepper
1 tablespoon fresh dill, chopped
8 ounces salmon, poached, skinned, boned, and flaked
1/2 cucumber, peeled, seeded, boned, and cubed
1 x 7-inch baked pastry shell

Pour the vinegar into a small bowl and sprinkle in the gelatin. Place the bowl over a pan of simmering water to dissolve the gelatin. In a larger bowl, combine the yogurt and mayonnaise. Season with salt and pepper to taste, then stir in the dill, vinegar, and gelatin. Add the salmon and cucumber and mix together well. Spoon into the pastry shell, level the surface and leave to set. Garnish with slices of cucumber.

Spinach Mushroom Tart
with Leeks & Italian Garden Vinaigrette

TART SHELL:

1 CUP FLOUR
1/2 TEASPOON SALT
4 TABLESPOONS COLD UNSALTED BUTTER, CUT INTO SMALL PIECES
1 1/2 TABLESPOONS SOLID VEGETABLE SHORTENING
2 1/2 TO 3 TABLESPOONS ICE WATER

Mix the flour and salt in a medium bowl. Add the butter and shortening and mix until the dough has the texture of coarse corn meal. Mix 2 1/2 tablespoons of ice water into the dough and shape into a ball. Add extra water if necessary to hold the dough together. Cover the ball with plastic wrap and let it rest in the refrigerator for at least 30 minutes. Preheat the oven to 425 degrees F. On a floured board, roll the dough into a circle approximately 1/8-inch thick. Place it in the tart pan, then trim the edges. Place the shell in the freezer for approximately 30 minutes or until it is firm. Cover the shell with pie weights. Bake in the oven for 10 minutes.

TART:

2 CUPS SPINACH, RINSED, WITH STEMS REMOVED
1 LARGE OR 2 SMALL LEEKS, FINELY CHOPPED (APPROXIMATELY 1 CUP)
2 TABLESPOONS ITALIAN GARDEN OLIVE OIL
1/4 POUND PORTABELLA MUSHROOMS, THINLY SLICED (APPROXIMATELY 1 CUP)
1/2 TEASPOON SALT
1 TEASPOON FRESH THYME, MINCED
3 LARGE EGGS
1 CUP CREAM
1/2 CUP GRATED GRUYERE CHEESE
FRESHLY GROUND BLACK PEPPER TO TASTE

Preheat the oven to 375 degrees F. Slice the spinach into thin ribbons. In a large pan, sauté the leeks in the oil over medium heat. When they are tender, add the mushrooms, salt, and thyme. After the mushrooms have given off juice and reabsorbed it, add the spinach leaves and stir until the leaves wilt. Cool the mixture. In a medium bowl, beat the eggs and add the cream and the cheese. Add the sautéed vegetables and taste for seasoning. Pour into the partially prebaked pie shell. Bake for 35 to 40 minutes or until the custard is firm and golden brown. Cool the tart for 20 to 30 minutes to allow it to settle and serve warm. Serves 4 to 8.

Shrimp & Vegetable Kebabs

with Ginger Lime Vinaigrette

Next time you have a cookout, try these fabulous shrimp and vegetable kebabs for a first course. Family and guests will have a great time threading their own skewers with lime-and-ginger-marinated shrimp and colorful summer vegetables. Lime is such a sprightly flavor, and just right for delicate seafood.

KEBABS:

1 1/4 SHRIMP
SELECTION OF PREPARED VEGETABLES, SUCH AS RED AND GREEN PEPPERS, ZUCCHINI, MUSHROOMS, CHERRY TOMATOES, ONIONS

MARINADE:

3 LIMES
1 TABLESPOON GINGER LIME VINEGAR
1 ONION, FINELY CHOPPED
1 TABLESPOON FRESH GINGER
1 LARGE CLOVE OF GARLIC, CRUSHED
3 TABLESPOONS OLIVE OIL

Finely grate the rind from one lime and squeeze the juice from all of them. Mix all the marinade ingredients together and pour over the shrimp. Stir gently, cover and refrigerate for 2 - 3 hours. Thread 4 skewers alternately with shrimp and vegetables. Cook slowly under a hot broiler or over a barbecue grill, basting occasionally with the marinade.

Texas Style Spicy Chicken Wings

with Hot Pepper Sauce

This recipe is an extra-spicy version of the American classic, owing to the Hot Pepper Sauce and Texas Style vinegar.

24 CHICKEN WINGS
1 TEASPOON SALT
1/4 TEASPOON FRESHLY GROUND PEPPER
4 CUPS VEGETABLE OIL FOR FRYING
1/4 CUP BUTTER
1/4 CUP HOT PEPPER SAUCE
1 TEASPOON TEXAS STYLE VINEGAR
BLUE CHEESE DRESSING

Remove wing tips and discard. Divide remaining wing in two parts at the joint, sprinkling with salt and pepper. Heat oil in deep fryer or skillet. Add half the wings and fry about 10 minutes or until golden brown and crisp, stirring occasionally. Remove with slotted spoon and drain on paper towels. Repeat with remainder of wings. Melt butter in a small saucepan over low heat, stir in pepper sauce and vinegar. Cook until thoroughly heated. Arrange wings on a platter and pour the sauce over the wings. Serve with the dressing for a dip.

Salmon Stuffed Rice Balls

with Pesto Vinaigrette

A jewel-like morsel of savory salmon is the surprising center in these pesto-flavored, deep fried rice balls. My little secret: you can speed the preparation of this recipe by using leftover risotto.

3 CUPS LIGHT CHICKEN OR VEGETABLE STOCK
2 TABLESPOONS PESTO VINEGAR
1 TABLESPOON OIL
1 SMALL ONION, VERY FINELY CHOPPED
1 1/2 CUP ARBORIO RICE
1 CUP BASIL LEAVES, CHOPPED
2 TABLESPOONS PINE NUTS, TOASTED
1 TABLESPOON FRESHLY GRATED PARMESAN CHEESE
1 EGG, BEATEN
SALT AND PEPPER
3 OUNCES SALMON, SKINNED, BONED, AND CUT INTO 18 CUBES
1 EGG, BEATED
1 CUP FRESH BREAD CRUMBS
VEGETABLE OIL FOR DEEP-FRYING

Heat the stock and vinegar in a pan and simmer gently. In another pan, heat the oil and cook the onion for 2 minutes, then stir in the rice. Cook, stirring, for another 2 minutes or until the rice is transparent. Stir in a ladleful of the hot stock and when it has been absorbed add another ladleful. Continue adding the stock, bit-by-bit, until the rice is tender. (Add extra vinegar if the liquid runs out.) Transfer the cooked rice to a bowl and leave to cool. Add the chopped basil, pine nuts, Parmesan and the egg to the rice. Mix and season well. With wet hands, shape the mixture into 18 balls, each about 1 1/2 inch in diameter. Make a hole in the side of each ball with your finger. Push a cube of salmon into the hole and then close it up. Dip each ball into the beaten egg, then roll in the bread crumbs. Deep-fry over a medium heat for 7 - 8 minutes, turning often. Drain well on paper towels.

Stuffed Mushrooms Florentine
with Italian Garden Vinaigrette

Your guests have never tasted baked mushrooms like these! Filled with a savory ham, spinach and cream cheese mixture enlivened by Italian Garden vinegar and olive oil, they are superb. Garnish with sprigs of fresh dill for added appeal.

8 LARGE FLAT MUSHROOMS
  ITALIAN GARDEN OLIVE OIL
6 OUNCES SPINACH, COOKED AND CHOPPED
2 OUNCES COOKED HAM, FINELY CHOPPED
2 OUNCES CREAM CHEESE
1 TABLESPOON ITALIAN GARDEN VINEGAR
  SALT AND PEPPER
1 TABLESPOON GRATED PARMESAN CHEESE
1 OUNCE FRESH BREADCRUMBS

Trim and wipe the mushrooms and brush lightly all over with the olive oil. Stand in an ovenproof dish. Combine the spinach, ham, cream cheese, and vinegar. Season with salt and pepper. Divide between the mushrooms. Combine the Parmesan and breadcrumbs, and sprinkle over the filled mushrooms. Cook uncovered for about 20 minutes at 400 degrees F. Serve hot.

Basic Vinaigrette

You will never run out of ideas for salad dressing recipes with this formula. It's easy to create new flavors using different combinations of infused olive oil and flavored vinegar. Custom design your dressing to suit each salad, light to hearty, mild to spicy.

4 TABLESPOONS GOURMET ART OF VERMONT FLAVORED VINEGAR
1 TEASPOON HONEY-DIJON MUSTARD
2 CLOVES GARLIC, MINCED
1 SHALLOT, MINCED
3/4 TEASPOON SALT
1/2 TEASPOON FRESHLY GROUND PEPPER
1/2 CUP GOURMET ART OF VERMONT OLIVE OIL
1 TABLESPOON CHIVES, CHOPPED
1 TABLESPOON ITALIAN PARSLEY, CHOPPED
1 TEASPOON OREGANO

Combine first 6 ingredients. Whisk in the olive oil until smooth. Add parsley, chives, and oregano. Salt and pepper to taste.

47

Tomatoes & Basil
with Maple Syrup Vinaigrette

I am often moved to try unusual flavor combinations I think will taste special, and this is one of my favorites. The marriage of basil and maple syrup is indeed a happy union, so tasty you will want crusty bread available to soak up every bit of dressing.

2 1/2 TO 3 POUNDS RIPE TOMATOES

VINAIGRETTE:
4 - 5 TABLESPOONS BASIL VINEGAR
3 TABLESPOONS MAPLE SYRUP
1 TEASPOON SALT
3/4 CUP BASIL OLIVE OIL
1/2 CUP FRESH BASIL LEAVES, CHOPPED
FRESHLY GROUND PEPPER

In a small bowl, whisk together vinegar, maple syrup, salt. Add the olive oil and basil leaves and blend well. Taste to adjust the seasonings. Slice the tomatoes into 1/4 inch slices and arrange on a platter. Pour the vinaigrette over the tomatoes and serve.

Tossed Salmon Salad

with Italian Garden Vinaigrette

What an inspired medley of tastes and textures, from satiny avocado to crunchy croutons. A glorious salad like this one is a meal in itself, especially for summer lunches.

1 CUP FRESH CROUTONS
4 TABLESPOONS PARMESAN CHEESE
1 HEAD CRISP LETTUCE, SHREDDED
1 SMALL BUNCH RADISHES, SLICED
1 AVOCADO, CUBED
12 OUNCES TO 1 POUND SALMON, POACHED, BONED, SKINNED, AND CUBED

VINAIGRETTE:

1 CLOVE GARLIC
SALT AND FRESHLY GROUND PEPPER
2 TEASPOONS ITALIAN GARDEN VINEGAR
3 TABLESPOONS ITALIAN GARDEN OLIVE OIL

Mix the croutons with the cheese in a small bowl. Assemble all the other ingredients in a large salad bowl. To make the vinaigrette, crush the garlic with salt, add freshly ground pepper and stir in the vinegar. Add the oil and whisk. Pour the dressing over the salad and toss gently. Finally, sprinkle with the croutons and cheese. Serve immediately.

Sliced Orange Beet Salad
with Cranberry Orange Vinaigrette

The word for this salad is "stunning." Overlapping slices of beet and orange provide gorgeous color, while toasted walnuts and a tasty Cranberry Orange dressing add wonderful flavor. Present this dish on a handsome platter at buffets so all can admire it.

4 POUNDS TRIMMED BEETS, COOKED, SLICED AND PATTED DRY
12 NAVEL ORANGES, PEELED AND SLICED
1 1/3 CUP WALNUTS, LIGHTLY TOASTED AND FINELY CHOPPED
3/4 CUP ORANGE JUICE
2 TABLESPOONS CRANBERRY ORANGE VINEGAR
1 TEASPOON SALT
3/4 CUP OLIVE OIL
GROUND PEPPER TO TASTE

Layer beets and orange slices in an overlapping pattern on a large serving platter. Sprinkle with walnuts. Whisk orange juice, vinegar and salt together in a small bowl. Add oil in a thin, steady stream, whisking constantly. Pour dressing over salad. Season with pepper.

Fresh Fennel Salad
with Italian Garden Vinaigrette

Fennel is native to the Mediterranean; in Italy they call it "finocchio." Its anise flavor and celery-like texture add a certain elegance to this variation of the classic Greek salad. I use spinach leaves instead of lettuce for their rich color, and lots of salty feta cheese. A wonderful dressing of Italian Garden olive oil and vinegar is the final delicious touch.

3 FENNEL BULBS, TRIMMED, SLICED
1 1/2 POUND CHERRY TOMATOES
1 CUCUMBER, PEELED AND SLICED
30 BLACK OLIVES
1/2 RED ONION
2 CUPS YOUNG SPINACH LEAVES, CLEANED, STEMS REMOVED
3 TABLESPOONS ITALIAN GARDEN OLIVE OIL
3 TABLESPOONS ITALIAN GARDEN VINEGAR
FRESHLY GROUND PEPPER
1 POUND FETA CHEESE

Put fennel, tomatoes, cucumber, olives, red onion slices, and spinach in a large salad bowl. Toss to mix. Beat the olive oil with the vinegar, add pepper to taste. Pour over salad and toss gently. Sprinkle with feta. Serve immediately.

Peppers Tricolore
with Fresh Basil Vinaigrette

Charring the peppers brings out all their special flavor, and makes them ready to absorb the dressing of Basil olive oil and vinegar. The combination of green, red and yellow peppers and sliced tomatoes creates a visual treat as well as a tasty one.

2 GREEN BELL PEPPERS
2 RED BELL PEPPERS
2 YELLOW BELL PEPPERS
6 TABLESPOONS BASIL OLIVE OIL
2 TABLESPOONS BASIL VINEGAR
2 CLOVES GARLIC, CRUSHED
SALT AND PEPPER TO TASTE
1 POUND TOMATOES
4 BASIL LEAVES, SHREDDED

Broil the peppers until the skin is blistered and charred, turning them so they blister all around. Place them in a plastic bag and set aside for 20 minutes. Peel off the skins, cut away the cores and discard the seeds. Slice the peppers and put them in a dish. Beat oil, vinegar, and garlic together. Season. Pour over the peppers and leave to marinate for 1 hour. Slice the tomatoes and arrange on a serving plate. Pile the peppers in the center and scatter the shredded basil leaves over.

58

Chilled Tortellini & Olive Salad

with Italian Garden Vinaigrette

Served warm or chilled, this lovely salad is a whole meal in a bowl: tender pasta studded with salami and mozzarella, olives and fresh basil, all wrapped up with Italian Garden dressing. I use tricolor tortellini for extra color and appeal.

8 OUNCES COOKED TORTELLINI, COOLED
1/2 CUP OLIVES, PITTED, CHOPPED
1 CUP SLICED SALAMI
1 CUP CUBED MOZARELLA CHEESE
1/2 CUP FRESH BASIL, CHOPPED
2/3 CUP ITALIAN GARDEN OLIVE OIL
1/3 CUP ITALIAN GARDEN VINEGAR
SALT AND FRESHLY GROUND PEPPER TO TASTE

Put the tortellini, olives, salami, cheese, and basil in a large serving bowl. Mix well. In a small bowl, combine olive oil, vinegar, salt and pepper. Pour over other ingredients. Stir. Serve immediately or chill in refrigerator for 1 hour before serving.

Summer Beet Salad
with Cranberry Orange Vinaigrette

Steamed young beets are dressed with olive oil and Cranberry Orange vinegar to create a wonderful little salad with big garden flavor and a brilliant red sauce.

3 CUPS BEETS, DICED
1 RED ONION, CHOPPED
1/2 CUP OLIVE OIL
1/3 CUP CRANBERRY ORANGE VINEGAR
1 TABLESPOON FRESH BASIL
SALT AND FRESHLY GROUND PEPPER TO TASTE

Steam beets until tender. Place beets and onions in a medium size bowl. In a small bowl, mix olive oil, vinegar, basil, salt and pepper to taste. Pour over beets and onions. Mix well. Serve immediately.

Fresh Tomatoes & Mozzarella
with Basil Olive Oil

For a new twist on an old favorite, I top this salad with toasted pine nuts. Be sure to toast them slowly over low heat; the delicate pine nuts burn easily. Remove them from the skillet as soon as they turn golden brown.

2 TABLESPOONS PINE NUTS, TOASTED
1 1/2 POUNDS TOMATOES
12 OUNCES MOZZARELLA CHEESE
2 TABLESPOONS BASIL LEAVES, CHOPPED
4 TABLESPOONS BASIL OLIVE OIL

Slice the tomatoes and cheese. Arrange on serving plates and season with salt and pepper. Sprinkle the basil leaves over the tomatoes and cheese. Drizzle the olive oil over all. Sprinkle with the toasted pine nuts.

Mixed Bean & Salmon Salad
with Thyme Lemon Vinaigrette

This cool, colorful salad is one I make often when early green beans are slender and crisp. If time is short you can substitute canned tuna for the fresh salmon, because the wonderful herbal flavors are the true key to success in this dish.

6 OUNCES GREEN BEANS
1 14 1/2 OUNCE CAN NAVY BEANS
1 RED ONION, HALVED AND THINLY SLICED
1 TABLESPOON CHOPPED OREGANO
2 TABLESPOONS CHOPPED PARSLEY
16 OUNCES SALMON FILLET, POACHED AND CHILLED
3 TABLESPOONS BASIL OLIVE OIL
2 TABLESPOONS THYME LEMON VINEGAR
1 CLOVE GARLIC, CRUSHED

Remove the ends from the beans and cook in a pan of salted water until crisp-tender. Drain. Rinse under cold water and drain again. Drain and rinse the navy beans. Put the green beans, navy beans, onion slices and herbs into a salad bowl. Skin the salmon and cut into bite-sized pieces. Carefully stir into the bowl. Whisk the olive oil, vinegar and garlic together and pour over the salad. Toss gently. Chill until ready to serve.

Panzanella

with Fresh Basil & Italian Garden Olive Oil

In the Old World spirit of Italian "peasant" cooking, this recipe is designed to make delicious use of stale bread. The popular Italian Garden olive oil and vinegar flavor enhancers add a special touch to a traditional dish.

1 POUND DAY-OLD ITALIAN BREAD, CUT INTO CUBES
1 1/2 POUNDS TOMATOES, CUBED
1 SMALL CUCUMBER, DICED
2 STALKS CELERY, CHOPPED
1 RED ONION, DICED
2 TABLESPOONS CAPERS
2 TABLESPOONS CHOPPED FRESH BASIL
1/2 CUP ITALIAN GARDEN OIL
1 1/2 TABLESPOONS ITALIAN GARDEN VINEGAR
SALT AND FRESHLY GROUND BLACK PEPPER TO TASTE

Soak bread cubes in cold water for 10 minutes, drain and squeeze dry. Combine bread, tomatoes, cucumber, celery, onion, capers and basil in a large bowl. Toss well. Whisk together oil and vinegar. Pour over salad. Toss again. Season to taste with salt and pepper. Serves 4.

Greek Island Salad
with Fresh Herbs and Basil Vinaigrette

I call this recipe "Greek Island Salad" because it brings the feeling of an Aegean summer to your table, whatever the time of year. The beauty of using Basil vinegar and olive oil infusions is that the flavor of fresh herbs is always at hand, even in the dead of winter.

1 POUND RIPE TOMATOES, CORED AND CUT INTO 1/2 INCH SLICES
2 TABLESPOONS CHOPPED CHIVES
1 SMALL RED ONION SLICED AND SEPARATED INTO RINGS
1/2 CUP BLACK OLIVES, PITTED AND CHOPPED
1 CUP FETA CHEESE, CRUMBLED
1/2 CUP BASIL VINEGAR
1 TEASPOON OREGANO
1 TEASPOON THYME
1/2 CUP BASIL OLIVE OIL
SALT AND FRESHLY GROUND PEPPER TO TASTE

Arrange tomato slices on a serving plate with the onion rings on the top. Sprinkle tomatoes with olives, chives and the feta cheese. In a small bowl, mix the vinegar, herbs, olive oil, salt and pepper. Pour over salad and serve.

Warm Spinach Salad
with Italian Garden Vinaigrette

Just a few minutes of cooking in Italian Garden olive oil and garlic gives fresh spinach a glossy deep green color and marvelous flavor. You can make this recipe even when no fresh herbs are available, because Zesty Dill vinegar is filled with the essence of summer herb flavor.

2 BUNCHES SPINACH, WASHED AND DRIED WITH
   STEMS REMOVED (APPROXIMATELY 8 CUPS)
4 TABLESPOONS ITALIAN GARDEN OLIVE OIL
4 CLOVES GARLIC, FINELY CHOPPED
2 TEASPOONS ZESTY DILL VINEGAR
SALT AND FRESHLY GROUND PEPPER

In a large pan, heat 2 tablespoons of the oil, add the garlic and stir for a few seconds. Add the spinach with the salt and sauté over medium heat for 3 to 5 minutes or until the greens have just wilted. Remove from the heat, add the remaining olive oil and the vinegar. Add salt and pepper to taste.

Grilled Vegetable Pasta Salad
with Herbed Hot Pepper Olive Oil

We all need a few last-minute dishes that can be made in a flash from ingredients that are easy to keep on hand. This colorful pasta salad is just such a recipe. I discovered that blending Hot Pepper olive oil with soup mix helps the vegetables brown beautifully. Do try it!

4 MEDIUM ZUCCHINI AND/OR YELLOW SQUASH, SLICED
1 MEDIUM SPANISH ONION, HALVED AND CUT INTO LARGE CHUNKS
1 ENVELOPE SAVORY HERB WITH GARLIC SOUP MIX
1/4 CUP HOT PEPPER OLIVE OIL
8 OUNCES ROTINI PASTA, COOKED AND DRAINED
3/4 CUP ROASTED RED PEPPERS, DICED
1/4 CUP SIMPLE PEPPER VINEGAR

Arrange zucchini, squash, and onion on a broiler pan. Brush with soup mix blended with the olive oil. Broil 5 minutes or until golden and crisp-tender. In a large bowl, toss pasta, vegetables, peppers, and vinegar. Stir. Serve warm or at room temperature.

Pear & Blue Cheese Salad

with Citrus Delight Vinaigrette

Bosc, Anjou and Bartlett pears work equally well in this recipe. Walnuts add delightful crunch to the silky pears, and the tangy citrus vinaigrette dressing sets off the sharp blue cheese flavor. Serve on a bed of crisp mixed greens.

2 TABLESPOONS OLIVE OIL
1 TABLESPOON CITRUS DELIGHT VINEGAR
1 TEASPOON DIJON MUSTARD
1/4 TEASPOON COARSELY GROUND PEPPER
2 MEDIUM PEARS, SLICED 1/4 INCH
2 TABLESPOONS BLUE CHEESE, CRUMBLED
2 TABLESPOONS WALNUTS, CHOPPED
2 TABLESPOONS PARSLEY, CHOPPED

In a medium bowl stir together all ingredients except the pears, blue cheese, walnuts and parsley. Add remaining ingredients; toss to coat.

Shrimp & Salmon Salad
with Cranberry Orange Vinaigrette

Turn ordinary mayonnaise into a spectacular dressing for seafood salad, simply by stirring in orange zest and Cranberry Orange vinegar. The orange flavor perfectly complements the shrimp and salmon, and the sauce has a lovely drape and pretty color. A sprinkling of toasted pine nuts is the finishing touch.

MAYONNAISE:

2 EGG YOLKS
1 TABLESPOON CRANBERRY ORANGE VINEGAR
1 TABLESPOON SUNFLOWER OIL
1 TABLESPOON ITALIAN GARDEN OLIVE OIL
GRATED ZEST OF ONE ORANGE

Beat the egg yolks and vinegar together. Beat constantly, adding the oil drop-by-drop. Be certain that the oil has been incorporated into the egg yolk before adding the next drop. When the mayonnaise starts to thicken and about half the oil has been used, start adding the oil more quickly, teaspoon-by-teaspoon. Season. Dilute, if necessary, with a few more drops of vinegar.

SALAD:

1 HEAD GREEN LETTUCE, SHREDDED
1 HEAD RADICCHIO, SHREDDED
1 POUND SALMON, POACHED, SKINNED, BONED AND CURED
12 OUNCES OF SHRIMP, DEFROSTED
3 CUPS HALVED MUSHROOMS
2 TABLESPOON PINE NUTS, TOASTED

Prepare the mayonnaise. Divide the lettuces between 4 bowls. Mix the salmon, shrimp, mushrooms, and mayonnaise together. Divide between the bowls and sprinkle with pine nuts.

80

Salmon Asparagus Pasta
with Italian Garden Vinaigrette

A dish to celebrate the first asparagus of the season, this salad is lovely when made with tricolor radiattore, the prettiest pasta of them all. Radiattore means little radiators, a charming example of Italian whimsy.

1 POUND SALMON FILLET
1 POUND ASPARAGUS, TRIMMED AND CUT INTO 2 INCH LENGTHS
1 POUND PASTA, SUCH AS RADIATORE
1/2 CUP ITALIAN GARDEN OIL
2 TABLESPOON ITALIAN GARDEN VINEGAR
SALT AND FRESHLY GROUND PEPPER TO TASTE
1/4 CUP FRESHLY GRATED PARMESAN CHEESE

Poach salmon until flesh is opaque and flakes easily, about 10 minutes. Remove skin and flake into large chunks. Set aside, covered. Cook pasta in boiling, salted water until tender, about 5 minutes. Set aside covered. Cook pasta in boiling, salted water until al dente, about 8 minutes. Drain, place in a large bowl and toss with oil, parsley and vinegar. Add reserved salmon and asparagus and toss again gently. Season to taste with salt and pepper. Serve with cheese. Serves 4.

Gazpacho

I treasure this recipe for the wonderful memories it evokes. When Kris and I lived in Germany, our host family entertained us with a festive picnic to which every guest contributed a dish. Some Spanish friends of theirs brought along the best Gazpacho I had ever tasted, and were kind enough to give me the recipe. Here it is, for you to enjoy at your next picnic.

1 1/2 POUNDS RIPE TOMATOES, BLANCHED, PEELED, SEEDED AND QUARTERED
1 GREEN BELL PEPPER, CORED, SEEDED AND CHOPPED
1 CUP CHOPPED CELERY
4 CUPS TOMATO JUICE
1/2 CUP GREEN ONIONS MINCED
5 TABLESPOON ITALIAN GARDEN VINEGAR
1 JALAPENO CHILE PEPPER
3 GARLIC CLOVES MINCED
SALT & PEPPER TO TASTE

Mix all ingredients together, chill over night. Garnish with dollop of sour cream and fresh basil leaves.

Tomato & Orange Soup
with Italian Vinaigrette

I like to serve this light, summery soup either at lunch time or as the first course for a dinner party. You will find it a very pretty soup, as well as a delicious one. Refreshing citrus, mellow tomato, and pungent basil combine to create a most intriguing flavor medley.

1 POUND TOMATOES, PEELED AND HALVED
1 ONION, SLICED
1 CARROT, SLICED
1 STRIP LEMON PEEL
1 BAY LEAF
2 TEASPOONS FRESH BASIL, CHOPPED
2 TABLESPOONS BASIL VINEGAR
2 1/2 CUPS VEGETABLE STOCK
2 TABLESPOONS BUTTER
1/4 CUP FLOUR
1 SMALL ORANGE

Squeeze the tomatoes to remove the seeds. Put the tomatoes, onion and carrot in a pan with the lemon peel, bay leaf and basil. Season. Add the stock and vinegar, and simmer, covered, for 30 minutes. Purée and set aside. Clean the pan, melt the butter, add the flour, and cook for a few minutes. Remove from the heat, then gradually add the puréed mixture. Bring to a boil to thicken. Peel the orange. Shred the peel finely and blanch, then refresh in cold water. Squeeze the orange and add the juice to the soup. Check the seasoning and serve garnished with orange peel.

Roasted Red Pepper Linguine

with Sundried Tomatoes & Basil Olive Oil

Pasta lovers will discover a new favorite sauce when they experience the intensely flavorful pairing of red peppers and sun-dried tomatoes, enriched with Basil olive oil and smoothed with white wine. With beautiful color, luscious taste, quick and easy preparation, this is an outstanding dish.

1 POUND LINGUINE COOKED, DRAINED
2 LARGE RED BELL PEPPERS
1/4 CUP BASIL OLIVE OIL
2 TEASPOONS FRESH BASIL, CHOPPED
1/3 CUP SUNDRIED TOMATOES PACKED IN OIL
1 SMALL ONION, CHOPPED
2 GARLIC CLOVES, MINCED
2 TEASPOONS FRESH PARSLEY
1/2 CUP WHITE WINE

Roast the peppers on the grill or under the broiler. Peel and chop coarsely. Sauté the onion and garlic in the olive oil until they are soft and golden in color. Add the remainder of the ingredients. Simmer 2 to 3 minutes. Pour over cooked linguine.

Lamb Ragù

with Italian Garden Oil and Vinegar

This flavorful, slow-cooked stew is a wonderful way to use up leftover lamb. It could be made with chicken or beef as well.

1 POUND LAMB STEW MEAT, CUBED
1 TABLESPOON ITALIAN GARDEN OIL
1 ONION, CHOPPED
3 CLOVES GARLIC, MINCED
3 16 OUNCES CANS DICED TOMATOES
1/2 CUP CHOPPED GREEN OLIVES WITH PIMIENTOS
1 TABLESPOON ITALIAN GARDEN VINEGAR
1 TABLESPOON CHOPPED ITALIAN PARSLEY
GRATED ZEST OF ONE LEMON
SALT AND FRESHLY GROUND BLACK PEPPER

In a large skillet, brown meat over medium heat. Drain and set aside. Wipe out skillet and return to heat. Add oil and onions and cook for 3 minutes, or until softened. Add garlic and cook 2 to 3 minutes, or until lightly browned. Add tomatoes, olives and vinegar. Bring to a boil, reduce heat to low and cook partially covered for at least 30 minutes. Just before serving, stir in parsley and lemon zest, and season to taste with salt and pepper. Serves 4.

Penne & Black Olives

with Basil Olive Sauce

In the middle of winter, when you are missing your herb garden, try this recipe for a super-quick, super-tasty pasta sauce. Basil olive oil and Pesto vinegar add all the flavor of garden fresh basil to sweet red onions and black olives.

1/4 CUP BASIL OLIVE OIL
2 RED ONIONS, HALVED AND SLICED
1 TEASPOON SUGAR
3 TABLESPOONS PESTO VINEGAR
2 HEAPING TABLESPOONS PITTED BLACK OLIVES, HALVED
SALT AND FRESHLY GROUND PEPPER
1 TABLESPOON BUTTER
1 TABLESPOON CHOPPED FRESH PARSLEY

Heat the oil in a heavy pan and stir in the onions to coat them with oil, then sprinkle with the sugar and cook for 5 minutes or until translucent. Add the vinegar and olives, season, and simmer for another 2 minutes. Remove from the heat and stir in the butter. Sprinkle with parsley, then check the seasoning and toss with hot pasta.

Goat Cheese & Prosciutto Spaghettini
with Italian Garden Olive Oil

This wonderful creamy sauce will remind you of an Alfredo sauce, but with the delightful difference of salty prosciutto and amazing ease of preparation. Spaghettini is the pasta of choice here. Notice that no fresh herbs are needed; Italian Garden infusions add the flavors of dill, rosemary and thyme.

2 TABLESPOONS ITALIAN GARDEN OLIVE OIL
2 SHALLOTS, MINCED
2 TABLESPOONS CHICKEN STOCK
2 TABLESPOONS ITALIAN GARDEN VINEGAR
6 OUNCES GOAT CHEESE, ANY RIND REMOVED, CUT INTO PIECES
2 OUNCES PROSCIUTTO, FINELY DICED
FRESHLY GROUND BLACK PEPPER
FRESHLY GRATED ROMANO CHEESE

Heat the oil in a heavy pan and gently fry the shallots until soft but not brown. Add the stock and vinegar, then the cheese, and mix together well. As soon as the cheese has melted, stir in the prosciutto and season with pepper. Toss with hot pasta and sprinkle with romano cheese.

Farfalle

with Porcini Mushroom Marinade

1 OUNCE DRIED PORCINI MUSHROOMS
2/3 CUP ITALIAN GARDEN VINEGAR
1 STICK (1/2 CUP) BUTTER
1 ONION, CHOPPED
1 CLOVE GARLIC, PEELED AND CRUSHED
1 TABLESPOON FRESH PARSLEY, CHOPPED
1 TABLESPOON FRESH BASIL LEAVES, CUT INTO STRIPS
1 TEASPOON TOMATO PASTE
1 POUND MIXED FRESH MUSHROOMS, ROUGHLY CHOPPED
SALT AND FRESHLY GROUND BLACK PEPPER
1 TABLESPOON FLOUR
1/2 CUP MEAT STOCK, PREFERABLY HOMEMADE
1 TEASPOON DIJON MUSTARD
FRESHLY GRATED PARMESAN CHEESE

Put the dried porcini in a bowl, cover with hot water, and let soak for 30 minutes. Drain, taking care to leave any grit from the porcini at the bottom of the bowl. Reserve 1/2 cup of liquid. In a small saucepan heat the vinegar and simmer for 4 minutes, then set aside. Melt half the butter in a heavy pan and gently cook the onion until soft but not browned. Add the garlic and herbs, and cook for 1 minute, then add the tomato paste and cook for 30 seconds more. Stir in the drained porcini and sauté for 5 minutes, then add the fresh mushrooms and cook over a medium heat for 5 minutes, turning the mushrooms regularly. Season, lower the heat, and cook for another 5 minutes. Meanwhile, melt the remaining butter in a heavy saucepan and mix in the flour. Remove the pan from the heat and carefully stir in the stock and the reserved porcini soaking liquid. Add the vinegar. Cook, stirring for 10 minutes. Stir in the mustard. Pour over the mushrooms and blend together well. Toss with hot pasta, season, and sprinkle with Parmesan.

Robust Chili Tomato Sauce Over Rotini

with Basil Vinaigrette

If you like your sauces bold and hot, this one will become a favorite. Chili pepper, anchovies and black olives give it the vibrant flavors of southern Italy, while Basil olive oil and vinegar add the herbal grace notes. Serve with a substantial pasta like rigatoni or penne.

2 TABLESPOONS BASIL OLIVE OIL

2 CLOVES GARLIC, PEELED AND MINCED

10 LARGE LEAVES FRESH BASIL, CHOPPED

1 FRESH HOT RED CHILI PEPPER, SEEDED AND MINCED

1 CAN (2 OUNCES) ANCHOVIES, DRAINED

1 1/3 CUPS ROUGHLY CHOPPED PITTED BLACK OLIVES

1/4 CUP BASIL VINEGAR

2 TABLESPOONS TOMATO PASTE

1 POUND RIPE TOMATOES, PEELED, SEEDED, AND CHOPPED

SALT AND FRESHLY GROUND BLACK PEPPER

FRESHLY GRATED PARMESAN CHEESE

Heat the oil in a heavy pan and gently fry the garlic, basil, and chili for 1 minute, taking care not to burn the garlic. Add the remaining ingredients, season, and simmer for 45 minutes, stirring occasionally. Toss with pasta and sprinkle with Parmesan.

Basil Scented Tuna

with Peppers and Olives

I recommend using solid white albacore tuna in this recipe for a very fancy tuna salad. Roasted peppers give the dish a Mediterranean accent, while Basil olive oil and vinegar impart the delicious taste of summer herbs. For those who prefer a milder flavor, the anchovy paste can be omitted.

4 BELL PEPPERS (RED, GREEN, OR ORANGE)
1 POUND TUNA CANNED IN WATER
3/4 CUP BASIL OLIVE OIL
1/2 CUP BASIL VINEGAR
1 STALK CELERY, CHOPPED
2 TABLESPOONS ANCHOVY PASTE
2 GARLIC CLOVES, MINCED
1/2 CUP OLIVES, PITTED AND HALVED
1/2 CUP ITALIAN PARSLEY
SALT AND FRESHLY GROUND PEPPER

Place whole peppers on a baking sheet and roast in a 400 degree F oven until the skins are evenly blackened. When cool, peel off the skins and cut into thin strips. Break the tuna into chunks. In a separate bowl, combine the oil, vinegar, celery, and anchovy paste. Stir in the peppers. Pour this mixture over the tuna and mix. Garnish with olives and parsley.

Zesty Dill Crabcakes
with Cantaloupe Pineapple Salsa

CRABCAKES:

2 EGG WHITES

2 TABLESPOONS HONEY-DIJON MUSTARD

1 TABLESPOON MAYONNAISE

1 TABLESPOON ZESTY DILL VINEGAR

1/2 TEASPOON SALT

1/4 TEASPOON FRESHLY GROUND BLACK PEPPER

1/8 TEASPOON RED SERRANO PEPPER

1/2 CUP FINE BREADCRUMBS

2 TABLESPOONS CHOPPED FRESH PARSLEY

1 POUND CRABMEAT

Prepare the salsa by combining the cantaloupe, pineapple, scallions, parsley, and vinegar in a small bowl. Refrigerate covered, for 3 hours or up to 2 days. Bring to room temperature before using.

Prepare the Crab Cakes by lightly beating together the egg whites, mustard, mayonnaise, vinegar, salt, pepper and red pepper in a medium-size bowl. Stir in the breadcrumbs and parsley until well mixed. Fold in the crabmeat. Gently shape mixture into 8 equal patties, about 3 inches in diameter. Place on a lightly greased broiler pan. Refrigerate at least 1 hour or up to 4 hours before broiling. Broil about 6 inches from heat for 5 minutes, or until cakes are browned on top and heated through to center.

Spoon the salsa over the crab cakes and serve immediately.

SALSA: SEE PAGE 15

Caribbean Lime Ginger Tuna

Why don't more cooks prepare fish on the outdoor grill? They would, if they had this recipe for a delightful sweet-sour marinade of Ginger Lime vinegar, honey, and mint. It's perfect for strong-flavored fish like tuna and swordfish, especially when served with Avocado, Lime & Tomato Salsa.

2/3 CUP GINGER LIME VINEGAR
1/3 CUP ORIENTAL OR WILDFLOWER HONEY
1/4 CUP SAFFLOWER OIL
1 TABLESPOON CHOPPED FRESH MINT
2 TABLESPOONS FRESHLY GRATED GINGER ROOT
2 GARLIC CLOVES, MINCED OR PRESSED
1 1/4 LB. TUNA STEAKS, CUT INTO 4 PIECES.

Combine marinade ingredients. Place marinade and fish in a large plastic bag and marinade for up to 1 hour in the refrigerator. Grill or broil fish for about 5 minutes per side, or until outside is brown and center is still pink. Discard marinade.

Savory Shrimp
with Almond Hot Pepper Pesto

Here's company fare your guests will be talking about for a long time: jumbo shrimp dressed with peppery almond-parsley pesto. I often serve this spicy recipe with a rice dish like risotto or pilaf, so not a drop of delicious sauce is lost.

1/4 CUP ALMONDS
2 CUPS LIGHTLY PACKED, RINSED AND DRAINED PARSLEY SPRIGS
1/3 CUP HOT PEPPER OLIVE OIL
3 TABLESPOONS SIMPLE PEPPER VINEGAR
1 CLOVE GARLIC
1 TABLESPOON CAPERS
SALT
1 POUND LARGE (31 TO 35 PER POUND) SHRIMP, SHELLED, DEVEINED, AND RINSED

In an 8-inch frying pan, stir the almond over medium heat until golden under the skin, about 8 minutes. Pour the almonds into a food processor; let cool. Add parsley, oil, vinegar, garlic, and capers. Whirl until smoothly pureed. Add salt to taste. In a 4- to 5-quart pan, bring 2 quarts of water to boiling on high heat. Add shrimp to pan, cover, and remove at once from heat. Let stand until shrimp are opaque in center (cut to test), about 2 to 3 minutes. Drain the shrimp and mound on a platter. Spoon sauce onto the warm shrimp. Makes 4 servings.

Oriental Lacquered Chicken

Everyone who tastes this succulent chicken dish asks for the recipe. The secret is in two sauces, a marinade of soy sauce and Ginger Lime vinegar that makes the chicken meltingly tender, and an Asian-inspired creation that adds complex, intriguing flavor and a shiny glaze.

MARINADE:

1 CUP LIGHT SOY SAUCE
1 CUP GINGER LIME VINEGAR
2 CLOVES GARLIC
1 TABLESPOON HONEY
2 TABLESPOONS CORNSTARCH
2 TEASPOONS FRESH GINGER

SAUCE:

1 CUP DRY WINE
1/2 CUP HOISIN SAUCE
1/2 CUP KETCHUP
2 CLOVES GARLIC, MINCED
1/4 CUP HONEY
1 TABLESPOON GINGER LIME VINEGAR
4 CHICKEN BREASTS, BONED AND SPLIT

Mix marinade and pour over chicken. Refrigerate covered for 6 hours, turning occasionally. Drain marinade and discard. Arrange chicken in baking dish. Combine sauce ingredients and pour half over the chicken. Bake at 375 degrees F for 25 minutes. Turn the chicken over and add the remaining sauce. Bake for another 25 minutes until tender, basting regularly during cooking time.

Savory Stuffed Tomatoes

4 LARGE TOMATOES
1 TABLESPOON BASIL OLIVE OIL
1 ONION, FINELY CHOPPED
1 CLOVE GARLIC, CRUSHED
1 STALK CELERY, FINELY CHOPPED
3/4 CUP BREAD CRUMBS
1 TABLESPOON OREGANO
SALT AND FRESHLY GROUND BLACK PEPPER

Stand tomatoes on their stem ends and slice off the top. Remove the pulp with a small spoon and reserve. Stand the tomatoes upside down on paper towels to drain. Heat the oil in a pan and fry the onion, garlic, and celery until soft but not browned. Stir in the bread crumbs, oregano and tomato pulp. Season well. Fill the tomato cases with the mixture and replace the top. Bake for about 20 minutes at 350 degrees F. Serve hot.

Roasted Rainbow Peppers

If the sweet, colorful peppers of summer tempt you to buy yellow, green, red, and orange ones by the bag full, here's what to do with them. This side dish, a rainbow of roasted peppers perked up with herbs and Hot Pepper olive oil and vinegar, makes even a plain hamburger fit for a king or queen.

2 EACH OF YELLOW, RED, GREEN AND ORANGE PEPPERS
3 TABLESPOONS SIMPLE PEPPER VINEGAR
3 TABLESPOONS HOT PEPPER OLIVE OIL
5 TABLESPOONS (TOTAL) OF PARSLEY, BASIL AND THYME
SALT AND FRESHLY GROUND PEPPER

Seed and chop peppers into large pieces. Place in an oven-proof dish. Mix vinegar, oil, and herbs and pour over peppers. Bake at 425 degrees F for 25 minutes. Serve hot.

Baked Chili Rice

To give my Chili rice a big Texas taste, I add Texas Style vinegar. An easy to prepare, one dish meal, this family favorite is a fine cold-weather supper featuring brown rice and ground beef.

1 1/2 POUNDS GROUND BEEF, BROWNED, DRAINED
2 SWEET ONIONS, CHOPPED
3 BELL PEPPERS, SEEDED AND CHOPPED
1 32 OUNCE CAN TOMATO SAUCE
1 SMALL JALAPEÑO CHILI
5 TABLESPOONS FRESH PARSLEY, BASIL, AND OREGANO, CHOPPED
2 TEASPOONS WORCESTERSHIRE SAUCE
1/3 CUP TEXAS STYLE VINEGAR
1 1/4 CUP UNCOOKED BROWN RICE

Combine all ingredients in a large oven-proof baking dish. Bake for 45 minutes at 350 degrees F.

Asparagus & Toasted Hazelnuts

2 POUNDS FRESH ASPARAGUS

1/4 CUP UNSALTED BUTTER

1/3 CUP Italian Garden OLIVE OIL

3/4 CUP TOASTED HAZELNUTS OR PINE NUTS

1/2 CUP Italian Garden VINEGAR

1 - 2 TEASPOONS MAPLE SYRUP

Lay asparagus in a large frying pan, cover with boiling salted water (about 2 inches) and cook uncovered 3 to 5 minutes, until crisp. Remove asparagus and plunge into cold water. Drain and pat dry. To prepare the vinaigrette, heat the butter and oil and add the nuts, maple syrup and vinegar. Cool. Pour over the asparagus. Season with salt and pepper, and serve immediately.

Beef Tenderloins

MUSHROOM MARINADE:

1/4 CUP PORCINI MUSHROOMS

3 TABLESPOONS COGNAC

2/3 CUP RED WINE

1/3 CUP PORCINI OLIVE OIL

2 TABLESPOONS SHALLOTS, CHOPPED

2 CLOVES GARLIC, PRESSED

1/2 TEASPOON OREGANO

1/2 TEASPOON BASIL

1 GENEROUS TABLESPOON HONEY

In a blender, grind the mushrooms fine to make about 2 tablespoons powder. Heat the cognac in a saucepan or microwave on high for 2 minutes. Stir the cognac into the mushroom powder to form a paste. Combine the mushroom paste and red wine in a nonreactive mixing bowl. Whisk in the oil a little at a time. Stir in the shallots, garlic, herbs, and honey.

BEEF:

4 BEEF FILETS, 6 OUNCES EACH, CUT ABOUT 1/2 INCH THICK

Place the beef in a nonreactive container or a 1-gallon zip lock bag. Pour the marinade over the beef and refrigerate for 6 to 8 hours. Remove the container from the refrigerator and let it stand covered for an hour at room temperature. Remove the beef from the marinade. To grill, lightly brush the grill with vegetable oil and sear the beef for 1 minute on each side. Continue grilling the beef: 5 to 6 minutes for rare or 7 to 8 minutes for medium rare, turning often.

Herbed Pork Roast

1 TABLESPOON FRESH PARSLEY

3 TABLESPOONS CRUSHED DRIED
BLACK PEPPERCORNS

1/4 CUP SOY SAUCE

1/4 CUP RED WINE

1/2 CUP GINGER LIME VINEGAR

ADD WATER AS NECESSARY

4 POUNDS LEAN PORK ROAST

2 TABLESPOONS HONEY-DIJON
MUSTARD

3 GARLIC CLOVES

2 ONIONS CUT IN HALF

Combine all ingredients except mustard. Place roast in marinade, refrigerate for 9 hours, turning occasionally. Drain and reserve marinade while you preheat oven to 325 degrees F. Spread mustard over roast. Put in oven and pour reserved marinade over pork. Bake 3 to 4 hours, until meat is heated through.

Spicy Red Cabbage

1 TABLESPOON VEGETABLE OIL

1 SMALL ONION, PEELED AND FINELY CHOPPED

1 1/2 POUND RED CABBAGE, TRIMMED AND FINELY SHREDDED

SALT AND PEPPER

2 TABLESPOONS BASIL VINEGAR

1 TABLESPOON BROWN SUGAR

1 APPLE, PEELED, CORED, AND CHOPPED

2 - 3 TABLESPOONS WATER

Heat the oil in an oven-proof casserole and fry the onion gently until soft but not colored. Add the cabbage and mix well, then season with salt and pepper. Add the vinegar, sugar, apple and water, and bring to a boil, stirring frequently. Cover the casserole tightly and cook in a 350 degree F oven for an hour. Stir well before serving piping hot.

Mashed Potatoes & Herbs

6 LARGE POTATOES

6 TABLESPOONS UNSALTED BUTTER

1 CUP HEAVY CREAM

3 TABLESPOONS ZESTY DILL VINEGAR

6 TABLESPOONS (TOTAL) FRESH PARSLEY, THYME, OREGANO, AND/OR DILL

Preheat oven to 400 degrees F. Place the potatoes on a baking sheet and bake until very tender, approximately 1 to 2 hours. Remove from oven and let cool slightly. Meanwhile, heat the cream and butter, and add the vinegar. Scoop the inside from the potatoes and mash in a bowl to the desired consistency. Stir in the cream and butter mixture and herbs. Season with salt and pepper, and serve immediately.

Apple Cranberry Crisp

TOPPING:

1/2 CUP PECAN HALVES, CHOPPED

1 CUP ALL-PURPOSE FLOUR

1/3 CUP LIGHT BROWN SUGAR

1/3 CUP GRANULATED SUGAR

1/4 TEASPOON GRATED ORANGE ZEST

1/3 CUP BUTTER, SOFTENED

FILLING:

6 DELICIOUS APPLES (APPROXIMATELY 2 POUNDS, PEELED, CORED, AND SLICED)

1 TABLESPOON GRANULATED SUGAR

1 TABLESPOON CRANBERRY ORANGE VINEGAR

Preheat the oven to 375 degrees F. In a large bowl, combine the dry ingredients and zest and work the softened butter in with your fingers. When the mixture resembles course sand, add the pecans and set aside. In a bowl, sprinkle the apples with the sugar and vinegar and mix with the dried cranberries. Place the filling into a baking dish, level, and spoon the topping evenly over the apples. Cover with foil and bake for 20 minutes. Remove the foil and continue baking for 20 minutes, or until the top is crisp and browned and apples are tender. Serve with ice cream.

Eve's Sweet Citrus Pecan Pie
with Cranberry Orange Zing

PIE CRUST:

1 1/4 CUP ALL PURPOSE FLOUR
8 TABLESPOONS UNSALTED BUTTER, CHILLED
PINCH OF SALT
1 TABLESPOON COLD CRANBERRY ORANGE VINEGAR
2 - 3 TABLESPOONS ICE COLD WATER

PIE FILLING:

6 TABLESPOONS UNSALTED BUTTER
4 LARGE EGGS
1/2 CUP LIGHT BROWN SUGAR
3/4 CUP GRANULATED SUGAR
1 TABLESPOON MAPLE SYRUP
2 TABLESPOONS CRANBERRY ORANGE VINEGAR
1 TEASPOON VANILLA
1 1/2 CUPS TOASTED PECANS
1 CUP WHIPPED CREAM WITH 2 TABLESPOONS OF SUGAR
1 CUP FRESH BERRIES

Mix flour, salt and butter in food processor. Pulse quickly several times, until the mixture is evenly blended. Add the vinegar and water, and pulse 6 times more. Press the dough together with your hands, wrap, and refrigerate for 2 hours. Roll out the dough between 2 sheets of parchment paper. Transfer to a 9-inch pie pan. Trim the edges. Cover the pie with parchment paper and fill with pie weights. Refrigerate the crust for 1 hour. Preheat the oven to 450 degrees F. Bake the pie crust for 15 minutes. Remove the cover and return to a 350 degree F oven for 10 - 15 more minutes, until lightly browned. Remove from the oven and cool.

For the filling, melt the butter and let cool. Beat the eggs until smooth and creamy. Add the sugar, vinegar, maple syrup, and vanilla, and beat well. Mix with the butter. Spread the pecans over the top of the baked pie crust. Pour the egg mixture over. Bake at 350 degrees F for 30 minutes. Remove from the oven and cool for 30 minutes. Garnish with whipped cream and fresh berries.

Tangy Watermelon
with Ginger Lime Zing

In summer when the watermelons are piled high at the market, buy a big one and try this unusual compote of melon and jicama, sparked with cilantro and piquant Ginger Lime vinegar. It's just the right dessert for a hot summer night.

2 MEDIUM JICAMA, PEELED AND CUT INTO 1/2 INCH CUBES
2 TABLESPOONS LIME JUICE
2 TABLESPOONS GINGER LIME VINEGAR
4 CUPS WATERMELON, SEEDED AND CUT INTO 1/2 INCH CUBES
1/2 CUP LOOSELY PACKED FRESH CILANTRO LEAVES, CHOPPED
LIME SLICES FOR GARNISH

Place jicama in a large bowl. Mix together the lime juice and vinegar. Pour over the jicama; cover and refrigerate for 30 minutes. When the jicama is chilled, add watermelon and cilantro; toss well. Cover and refrigerate 15 minutes longer to allow flavors to blend. Garnish with lime slices.

Citrus Scented Pound Cake

Here's a new twist on an old favorite. Rich, dense poundcake is enlivened with lemon extract and the merest suggestion of Citrus Delight vinegar. Cut in very thin slices and relish the delicious difference these flavorings make.

3 CUPS FLOUR
2 CUPS WHITE SUGAR
1/2 TEASPOON SALT
1 TEASPOON BAKING POWDER
1 1/2 CUPS SALTED BUTTER, SOFTENED
1/3 CUP MILK
6 LARGE EGGS
1 TEASPOON PURE LEMON EXTRACT
1 TEASPOON CITRUS DELIGHT VINEGAR
2 TABLESPOONS CONFECTIONERS' SUGAR, SIFTED

Preheat oven to 350 degrees F. Grease and flour a bundt pan. In a large bowl with an electric mixer on low speed, blend flour, sugar, salt and baking powder. Add butter, milk and 3 eggs. Beat on low until dry ingredients are moistened. Increase speed to high and beat for 2 minutes. Scrape down sides of bowl. Add lemon extract and vinegar, and blend at medium speed. Add the remaining 3 eggs one at a time, beating at high speed for 30 seconds after each addition. Pour batter into prepared pan, and bake 50 - 60 minutes or until a toothpick inserted into the cake comes out clean. When cake is done, cool in pan 15 minutes, then invert on a cooling rack. Cool to room temperature, then dust with confectioners' sugar.

Raspberry Mint Cooler
with Cranberry Orange Zing

When you don't want alcohol in your after-dinner drink, enjoy this refreshing blender beverage, so pretty in a frosty tall glass. Just a hint of Cranberry Orange vinegar brings out all the fresh flavor of ruby raspberries, cooled with club soda and a mint leaf garnish.

6 CUPS FRESH RASPBERRIES
1 3/4 CUPS CRANBERRY ORANGE VINEGAR
2 1/2 CUPS SUGAR
ICE CUBES
24 FRESH MINT LEAVES
6 CUPS CHILLED CLUB SODA

Place half of the berries in a large glass bowl. Pour 1 1/4 cups vinegar over. Cover and let stand 24 hours at room temperature. Strain mixture through a sieve set over a bowl, pressing on solids with the back of a spoon to release as much pulp as possible. Add remaining berries and 1/2 cup vinegar. Cover; let stand 24 hours at room temperature. Strain mixture through a sieve set over a large heavy saucepan, pressing on solids. Add sugar; stir over medium-high heat until sugar dissolves. Boil until reduced to 2 3/4 cups, about 10 minutes. Pour mixture into a glass bottle or jar; refrigerate. Seal. (Can be made 1 month ahead. Store in dark place at room temperature.) Fill 8 glasses with ice. Add 3 mint leaves, 3 tablespoons raspberry mixture and 3/4 cup club soda to each glass. Stir. Garnish with mint.

Fresh Cherry Pie
with Cranberry Orange Zing

There's only one crust on this fresh cherry dessert, so it's twice as easy as pie, and tastier, too. Orange juice in the filling and Cranberry Orange vinegar in both filling and crust add a most intriguing layer of flavor. Top with vanilla frozen yogurt for a special treat.

8 CUPS PITTED FRESH SWEET CHERRIES (ABOUT 4 POUNDS)
1 3/4 CUPS ALL PURPOSE FLOUR
3/4 CUP PLUS 3 TABLESPOONS SUGAR
1 TEASPOON ORANGE JUICE
2 TEASPOONS CRANBERRY ORANGE VINEGAR
1/2 CUP (1 STICK) CHILLED UNSALTED BUTTER, CUT INTO PIECES
1 LARGE EGG
2 TABLESPOONS ORANGE JUICE
1 TABLESPOON CRANBERRY ORANGE VINEGAR
1/4 TEASPOON SALT

Preheat oven to 400 degrees F. Mix cherries, 1/4 cup flour, 3/4 cup sugar, orange juice and vinegar in a large bowl. Transfer mixture to an 8-inch square glass baking dish. Combine 1 1/2 cups flour, 2 tablespoons sugar, butter, egg, orange juice, vinegar and salt in processor. Using on/off turns, process until clumps form. Turn out onto floured surface; knead until dough comes together. Roll out on a floured surface to 11-inch square. Place atop filling. Fold edges over, forming double thick edge. Crimp edge. Sprinkle with 1 tablespoon sugar. Cut vents in the crust to allow steam to escape. Bake until juices bubble and crust is golden, about 50 minutes. Serve warm or at room temperature.

ACKNOWLEDGEMENTS

I would like
to offer my
sincere thanks
to the many
individuals
w h o s e
contributions
were vital to
this project's
complete success.
First and foremost, I
thank my husband Kris,
whose unwavering support, love
and dedication to this endeavor make
him my true partner and best friend. To
my young children, Patrick and Martha, who
bring a special joy and tenderness to my
otherwise hectic world. To my business
partners, graphic designer David Griffin and
book producer Gary Chassman. And to my
many friends who have shared one
common characteristic: their belief that
my dream was indeed possible and my
idea worth pursuing. To all of you
who have shared my passion,
I give you my heartfelt thanks.

Eve Plociennik

Library of Congress Cataloging in Publication Data

Plociennik, Eve, 1959
A passion for flavor: cooking with infused oil and vinegar/Eve Plociennik
1. Plociennik, Eve, 1959

First Edition
10 9 8 7 6 5 4 3 2 1

Printed in Italy

Photography: Len Mastri
Recipe Styling: Melissa McClelland
Copy: Rita Randazzo
Copy Editor: Melinda Meyer
Design: David Griffin

*For information about quantity purchases
of this book, or any other questions regarding
this book, please contact the publisher
at the following address:*

Verve Editions
431 Pine Street
Burlington, Vermont 05401
e-mail vervevt@aol.com

Produced by